A New True Book

MOON FLIGHTS

By Dennis B. Fradin

CHILDRENS PRESS ™

CHICAGO

Eratosthenes Crater

PHOTO CREDITS

NASA—Cover, 4 (top), 11, 12 (2 photos), 13, 17 (2 photos), 29, 32, 33, 36, 41, 44

Smithsonian Institution: National Air & Space Museum—18 (bottom)

Holiday Film Corporation—2, 14, 15, 18 (top), 20, 22, 25, 27, 31 (right), 34, 35 (2 photos), 38 (2 photos), 40, 42 (2 photos)

The Granger Collection—6, 8, 10, 11, 31 (left)

Len Meents—4 (bottom)

COVER: Astronaut James B. Irwin salutes the flag. The lunar lander is in the center and the lunar rover is on the right.

For Rebecca Fradin Polster

Library of Congress Cataloging in Publication Data

Fradin, Dennis B.
  Moon flights.

  (A New true book)
  Includes index.
  Summary: Describes man's first landing on the moon, later moon walks in Project Apollo, and the importance of these missions to our exploration of space.
    1. Project Apollo—Juvenile literature. [1. Project Apollo. 2. Space flight to the moon] I. Title.
TL789.8.U6A5335   1985   629.45′4   84-23154
ISBN 0-516-01940-6   AACR2

TABLE OF CONTENTS

Full moon photographed from an Apollo spacecraft.

MOON

EARTH

OUR NEAREST NEIGHBOR IN SPACE

The moon is the nearest heavenly body to our planet, the earth. The moon orbits the earth at a distance of about 240,000 miles. That's quite a distance! Yet the other planets are millions of miles away. And the stars are many *trillions* of miles from the earth.

People always have thought about visiting the moon. Nearly two thousand years ago a Greek named Lucian wrote stories about moon voyages. During the late 1800s the Frenchman

Engraving from Jules Verne's *From the Earth to the Moon*

Jules Verne wrote *From the Earth to the Moon*. In his book the space travelers were shot to the moon by a giant cannon!

Until recently, one force of nature prevented real moon voyages. That force is gravity—the force that holds things down to heavenly bodies. When a ball is thrown into the air, gravity returns it to the ground. The only way to overcome gravity is to move very fast. For

The first heavier-than-air flight of the Wright Brothers
took place at Kitty Hawk, North Carolina on December 17, 1903.
Orville Wright flew the plane. Wilbur Wright stayed on the ground.

example, a ship bound for the moon must go at least 24,300 miles per hour to break away from the earth's gravity.

The first flying machines went less than one hundred miles per hour.

Even the jets of later years flew only about five hundred miles per hour. To reach the moon, something stronger was needed.

Scientists thought that powerful engines called rockets could do the job. In 1926 the American scientist Robert H. Goddard made the first modern rocket launch. His rocket went only sixty

On March 16, 1926, at Auburn, Massachusetts, Robert H. Goddard (1882-1945) launched the first liquid propellant rocket (left). Robert Goddard (fourth from left) and his assistants L. Mansur, A. Kisk, C. Mansur, and N.L. Jungquist hold the rocket launched on April 19, 1932 at Roswell, New Mexico.

miles per hour. But by the late 1950s both the United States and Russia had built rockets that could go at least 24,300 miles per hour—fast enough to travel to the moon.

A Saturn V rocket, topped by the Skylab space station, lifts off.

Scientists decided to launch probes before sending people to the moon. Probes are devices that send back information from outer space. On September 12, 1959, Russia launched *Luna 2,*

The *Ranger IV* space probe (left) that photographed the lunar surface was launched by an Atlas-Agena rocket (right).

the first probe to land on the moon. The first U.S. probe to reach the moon was *Ranger IV*, launched on April 23, 1962. During the next few years the U.S. and Russia sent more than

Spacesuits worn by the astronauts are displayed at the Johnson Space Center.

twenty other probes that either landed on or came close to the moon.

Scientists learned much from the moon probes. For example, the probes proved the moon has neither air nor water. They also proved objects could be landed safely on the moon.

The United States was the only nation to land astronauts on the moon.

By the mid-1960s scientists were talking of landing people on the moon. Russia thought it was too dangerous and costly to try. But the U.S. decided to do it. The date for blast-off was set: July 16, 1969.

PLANNING THE FIRST MOON WALK

Three astronauts were chosen to make the first moon landing. They were Neil A. Armstrong, Edwin E. ("Buzz") Aldrin, Jr., and Michael Collins.

Neil A. Armstrong, Michael Collins, and Edwin E. "Buzz" Aldrin

Armstrong, the mission commander, was a former fighter pilot and test pilot. Aldrin was a former fighter pilot. Collins had been an air force officer.

The vehicle that would take the astronauts to the moon was an Apollo spacecraft. Since the U.S. had built ten previous Apollos, this one was called *Apollo 11.*

The *Apollo 11* was supplied with air, water,

PEAS ORANGE DRINK COCOA

BEEF SALMON SALAD PEACHES

DATE FRUIT CAKE BEEF SANDWICHES CHEESE SANDWICHES STRAWBERRY CUBES

Because there is no pull of gravity in space, all foods must be dried and put in plastic containers. The earth-meal (bottom right) can be processed to fit in the four plastic bags shown at the top of the picture.

and freeze-dried food.
Space suits would provide
the astronauts with air and
keep their bodies at a
normal temperature when
they walked on the moon.

17

A Saturn rocket (above) carried Apollo's command module *Columbia* (below) and the lunar module *Eagle* into space.

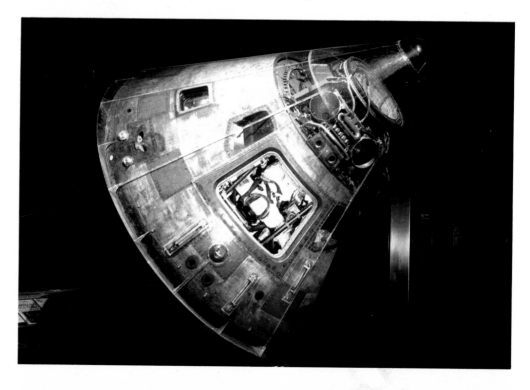

A TV camera also was sent along. It would enable millions of people back on the earth to see the first moon walk.

The *Apollo 11* would carry the three astronauts close to the moon. The craft would then split into two parts—the command module *(Columbia)* and the lunar module *(Eagle)*. *Columbia* would orbit the moon with Collins inside.

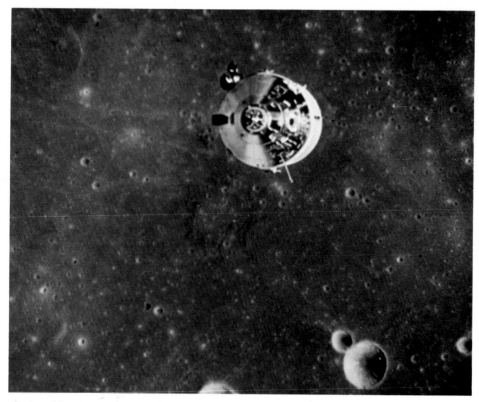

Columbia, the command module, orbited the moon while Armstrong and Aldrin explored the lunar surface.

Armstrong and Aldrin would get into *Eagle,* which would blast away from *Columbia* and land on the moon.

After exploring the moon,
Armstrong and Aldrin
would blast off in *Eagle*
and dock with *Columbia*.
The three astronauts would
then return to the earth in
Columbia.

This was how events
were to unfold—*if* the
mission went as planned.
But if something went
wrong, the mission could
end in disaster.

THE FIRST MOON WALK

On July 16, 1969, more than a million people were at Cape Kennedy (now called Cape Canaveral), Florida, to watch the launch. At 9:32 A.M. Florida time, *Apollo 11* blasted off into the blue sky.

Within twelve minutes of blast-off, the spacecraft had reached 17,400 miles per hour at a height of 119 miles. Several hours

later the ship was traveling
about 24,300 miles per
hour—fast enough for it to
break loose from the
earth's gravity.

"That Saturn (the name
of the rocket that carried
Apollo 11 into space) gave
us a magnificent ride,"
Commander Armstrong
reported.

"It looks like you are
well on your way now,"
ground control answered.

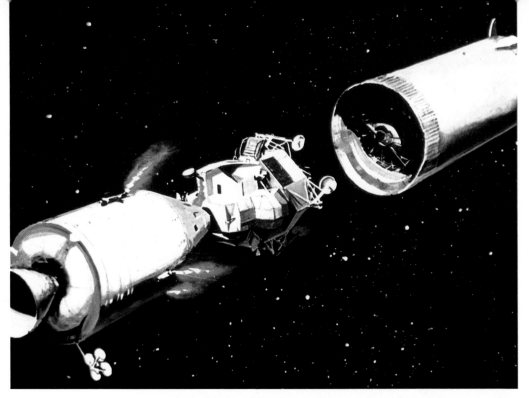

Artist's drawing shows the command module separating from the third stage of the Saturn rocket.

Three days later, *Apollo 11* went into orbit around the moon. Armstrong and Aldrin then climbed into the lunar module *Eagle*. Early on the afternoon of July 20, 1969, *Eagle* separated from the command module and headed down to the moon.

Very near the lunar surface, Commander Armstrong spotted trouble. The computer was about to bring *Eagle* down into a cluster of boulders! Commander Armstrong took control of the *Eagle* from the computer. At 4:17 P.M. on July 20, he brought *Eagle* down onto a smooth area.

This photograph taken from the *Columbia* shows the lunar module, *Eagle,* over the moon. The earth can be seen in the background.

"The *Eagle* has landed!" Armstrong reported, as he and Aldrin became the first human beings to reach the moon.

27

Armstrong and Aldrin checked over the *Eagle* for the next several hours. They also ate the first meal on the moon. Then Commander Armstrong prepared for one of the greatest moments in history. Wearing his space suit, he opened the lunar module's hatch. At 10:56 P.M. on July 20, 1969, he placed his left foot on the moon.

Neil Armstrong, photographed "Buzz" Aldrin climbing down from the *Eagle.*

"That's one small step for man, one giant leap for mankind," Armstrong said, as half a billion people on earth watched on television.

Eighteen minutes later Aldrin left the *Eagle* and joined Armstrong. The two astronauts scooped up moon rocks and set up several instruments. They also planted an American flag in the soil and unveiled a plaque that said:

Here men from the planet earth first set foot on the moon, July 1969 A.D. We came in peace for all mankind.

After a two-hour moon walk the two returned to *Eagle*. Then came a crucial moment—the lift-off.

The memorial plaque (above) was left on the moon. A solar wind sheet (left) was set up to collect atomic particles from the sun.

If *Eagle's* engine failed, the men would be stranded on the moon.

The lift-off was smooth. *Eagle* docked with *Columbia* and the

The *Columbia* landed in the Pacific Ocean.

astronauts spent the next three days returning to the earth. On July 24, 1969, *Columbia* splashed down in the Pacific Ocean. The rescue of the three astronauts from the ocean provided a happy finish to the mission.

LATER MOON WALKS

Because it came first,
the *Apollo 11* mission is
the most famous manned
moon landing. But during
the next several years U.S.
astronauts landed on the
moon five more times.

THE MOON WALKS

Name of Mission	Date of Mission	Astronauts Who Walked on the Moon
Apollo 11	July 16-24, 1969	Neil A. Armstrong and Edwin E. Aldrin, Jr.
Apollo 12	November 14-24, 1969	Charles Conrad, Jr., and Alan L. Bean
Apollo 14	January 31-February 9, 1971	Alan B. Shepard, Jr., and Edgar D. Mitchell
Apollo 15	July 26-August 7, 1971	David R. Scott and James B. Irwin
Apollo 16	April 16-27, 1972	John W. Young and Charles M. Duke, Jr.
Apollo 17	December 7-19, 1972	Eugene A. Cernan and Harrison H. Schmitt

Hundreds of people at mission control stations aided the crews of the Apollo missions.

Gulf of Mexico (above) photographed by Apollo.
Specially designed heat shields protected *Columbia* from
burning up upon re-entry into the earth's atmosphere.

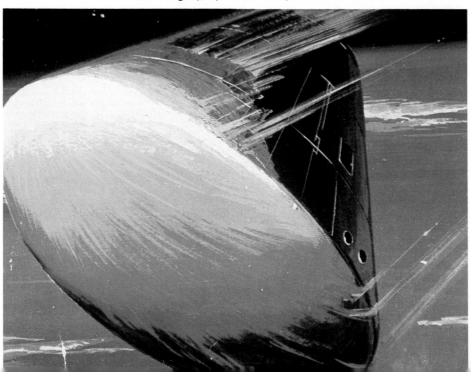

The lunar rover explored the moon's surface.

In the later missions, the astronauts got to ride as well as walk on the moon. During the *Apollo 15* mission astronauts David R. Scott and James B. Irwin became the first to explore in a lunar rover. The vehicle took the astronauts farther than they could have gone by walking.

Close-up of a lunar crater (above). When Neil Armstrong took this picture of "Buzz" Aldrin, he also took his own picture. Look at the face plate on Aldrin's helmet.

The twelve astronauts who reached the moon gathered hundreds of pounds of rocks and soil, which they brought back to earth. They took thousands of moon pictures and did many experiments.

WHAT WAS LEARNED?

From the six missions scientists learned that although the moon lacks water and air, it is like the earth in some ways. Like the earth, the moon underwent great volcanic activity long ago. Also like the earth, the moon is divided into three main parts: core, mantle, and crust. Tests of rocks

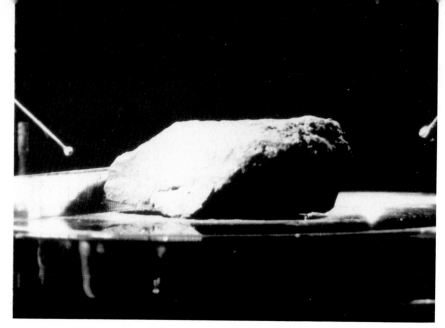

Moon rock

brought back by *Apollo 17* showed that the moon is the same age as the earth—about 4.6 billion years old. This means the earth and the moon (and probably the rest of our solar system) were formed at the same time.

All the astronauts who explored the moon returned to earth safely and in good health.

The moon walks also proved that people can work well on another world. This was good news for those who want to see more trips to other bodies in outer space.

When the Apollo astronauts returned to earth they wore
special suits and helmets and were quarantined (above). They were
kept from other people while doctors checked them to make
sure they did not bring back any diseases from the moon.

FUTURE VOYAGES
TO OTHER WORLDS

After the sixth moon walk in December of 1972, the Apollo moon-landing program ended. In the future, though, people probably will make more trips to the moon. Bases even may be built so that people can stay there for weeks at a time.

Some scientists think that the moon could be

The earth appears in the distance above the antenna of the lunar rover.

used as a pad for launching rockets into deep space. Because the moon has so little gravity, it would be easier to launch rockets from there than it is from the earth. Perhaps we will see the day when the moon is the jumping-off place for rockets headed to Venus or Mars. Or the day when a trip to the moon is as easy as a short car trip is today!

WORDS YOU SHOULD KNOW

Apollo 11(uh•POL•oh)—The spacecraft that transported the first moon visitors

astronauts(AST•roh•nawts)—American space travelers

billion(BILL•yun)—a thousand million (1,000,000,000)

command module(kuh•MAND MOD•jool)—the part of the Apollo spacecraft that remained in orbit around the moon while the astronauts landed in the lunar module

data(DAY•ta)—information

experiments(ex•PEHR•ih•ments)—tests made by scientists to check theories or discover facts

gravity(GRAV•ih•tee)—the force that holds things down to the earth and other heavenly bodies

lunar(LOON•er)—relating to the moon

lunar module(Loon•er MOD•jool)—the part of the Apollo spacecraft that landed on the moon

lunar rover(LOON•er ROH•ver)—a vehicle used to transport astronauts across the moon's surface

million(MILL•yun)—a thousand thousand (1,000,000)

orbit(OR•bit)—the path an object takes when it moves around another object

plaque(PLAK)—a marker left in a place to commemorate an event

rocket(ROCK•it)—a powerful engine used to propel a spacecraft

solar system(SOH•ler SISS•tim)—the sun and all objects orbiting it

space(SPAISS)—the region that begins about one hundred miles above the earth

space probes(SPAISS PROHBZ)—devices that send back information from outer space

space suits(SPAISS SOOTS)—protective, oxygen-equipped suits worn by astronauts when they leave their spacecraft

trillion(TRILL•yun)—a thousand billion (1,000,000,000,000)

volcanic(vol•CAN•ick)—relating to volcanoes

INDEX

About the Author

Dennis Fradin attended Northwestern University on a partial creative writing scholarship and graduated in 1967. He has published stories and articles in such places as Ingenue, The Saturday Evening Post, Scholastic, Chicago, Oui, *and* National Humane Review. *His previous books include the Young People's Stories of Our States series for Childrens Press, and* Bad Luck Tony *for Prentice-Hall. In the True book series Dennis has written about astronomy, farming, comets, archaeology, movies, and the space lab. He is married and the father of three children.*